Environmental Science

Study Guide

HOLT McDOUGAL

 HOUGHTON MIFFLIN HARCOURT

TO THE STUDENT

These Study Guide worksheets can be used in several ways to guide you through your textbook. The worksheets can be used as a pre-reading guide to help you identify the main concepts of each chapter before your initial reading. You can also use the worksheets after reading each chapter to test your understanding of the chapter's main concepts and terminology. Finally, you can use the worksheets to prepare for your environmental science exams. Regardless of how you and your teacher use the *Holt McDougal Environmental Science Study Guide*, it will help you determine which topics you have learned well and which topics you need to study further.

PHOTO CREDITS

Cover, title page: *tree* ©Douglas Waters/The Image Bank/Getty Images.
Cover: *honeycomb* ©Brian Hagiwara/Foodpix/Getty Images; *bees* ©Old Dog Photography/Flickr/Getty Images; *rain forest* ©altrendo nature/Getty Images; *turtles* ©Flickr/Getty Images; *greenhouse* ©Nigel Cattlin/Photo Researchers, Inc.; *arctic* ©Arctic-Images/The Image Bank/Getty Images; *storm chaser* ©Ryan McGinnis/Flickr Select/Getty Images.

Contents

Chapter 1: Science and the Environment
Study Guide

MATCHING

In the space provided, write the letter of the description that best matches the term or phrase.

_____ 1. practice of growing, breeding, and caring for plants and animals used for a variety of purposes

_____ 2. study of how living things interact with each other and with their nonliving environments

_____ 3. conflict between short-term interests of individuals and long-term welfare of society

_____ 4. declining number and variety of the species in an area

_____ 5. field of study involving the physical, biological, and social sciences.

_____ 6. law describing the relationship between an item's availability and its value.

_____ 7. characterized by low population growth rate, high life expectancy, and diverse industrial economies

_____ 8. characterized by high population growth rate, low energy use, and very low personal wealth

_____ 9. state in which a human population can survive indefinitely

_____ 10. natural material that can be replaced relatively quickly through natural processes

a. loss of biodiversity

b. supply and demand

c. "The Tragedy of the Commons"

d. agriculture

e. developed nation

f. environmental science

g. ecology

h. developing nation

i. renewable resource

j. sustainability

MULTIPLE CHOICE

In the space provided, write the letter of the term or phrase that best completes each statement or best answers each question.

_____ 11. Which of the following sciences contribute to the field of environmental science?
  a. physics and chemistry
  b. biology and earth science
  c. social sciences
  d. all of the above

_____ **12.** All of the following make up the three major categories of
environmental problems *except*
    a. loss of biodiversity.   **c**. resource depletion.
    b. overpopulation.   **d**. pollution.

_____ **13.** During the period of human history known as the _____, human
populations grew rapidly because of advances in farming methods.
    a. Industrial Revolution   **c.** "Tragedy of the Commons"
    b. agricultural revolution   **d.** hunter-gatherer period

_____ **14.** Which major changes in human society and the environment occurred
during the Industrial Revolution?
    a. People lived in small tribes; many mammals went extinct.
    b. Domesticated plants were altered; forest was replaced
with farmland.
    c. Fossil fuel consumption, technological efficiency, and
environmental pollution increased.
    d. Common grazing areas were replaced with closed fields.

_____ **15.** What did hunter-gatherers do to alter the environment?
    a. introduce plants to new   **c.** burn prairie to maintain
regions   grassland
    b. overhunt large mammals   **d.** all of the above

_____ **16.** Developed nations make up about _____ percent of the world's
population and consume about _____ percent of its resources.
    a. 20, 75   **c.** 75, 20
    b. 50, 75   **d.** 75, 50

_____ **17.** Hardin's "Tragedy of the Commons" essay addressed the conflicts
associated with which environmental challenge?
    a. preventing pollution   **c.** curbing overpopulation
    b. preserving biodiversity   **d.** protecting shared resources

_____ **18.** The ecological footprint for a person in a particular country takes into
account what requirements of supporting that individual?
    a. land used for crops   **c.** forest area that absorbs pollution
    b. land taken up by housing   **d.** all of the above

_____ **19.** Attempts to create a sustainable society strive to achieve what?
    a. greater resource consumption   **c.** negative population growth
    b. stable resource consumption   **d.** restrictions on technology

_____ **20.** A cost-benefit analysis balances the cost of an action against
    a. those who benefit from the action.
    b. those who perform the analysis.
    c. what consumers and taxpayers are willing to pay.
    d. the benefits one expects to receive.

Chapter 2: Tools of Environmental Science
Study Guide

MATCHING

In the space provided, write the letter of the description that best matches the term or phrase.

_____ **1.** control group

_____ **2.** prediction

_____ **3.** physical model

_____ **4.** risk

_____ **5.** conceptual model

_____ **6.** value

_____ **7.** experiment

_____ **8.** statistics

_____ **9.** data

a. a logical statement about what will happen in an experiment

b. a verbal or graphical explanation for how a system works or how it is organized

c. in an experiment, that which does not receive the experimental treatment

d. a three-dimensional model you can touch

e. principles or standards considered to be important

f. the probability of an unwanted outcome

g. information gathered during an experiment

h. procedure designed to test a hypothesis

i. collection and classification of data

MULTIPLE CHOICE

Choose the best response. Write the letter of that choice in the space provided.

_____ **10.** When it is not possible to conduct an experiment, scientists test their predictions by
    a. examining correlations.
    b. using a control.
    c. testing for one variable.
    d. remaining skeptical.

_____ **11.** An essential feature of every good experiment is that it should
    a. use a control.
    b. test a single variable.
    c. graph data.
    d. both (a) and (b)

_____ **12.** Experimental methods include which of the following steps?
    a. remaining skeptical, organizing data, and analyzing data
    b. drawing conclusions, being open to new ideas, and communicating results
    c. observing, hypothesizing, predicting, experimenting, and communicating results
    d. being curious, imagining, being able to see patterns, observing, and predicting

_____ **13.** What is not a description of a good hypothesis?
    a. It makes logical sense.
    b. It is a testable explanation of an observation.
    c. It follows from what you already know about a situation.
    d. It is a guess based on previous experiments.

Name _____ Class _____ Date _____

Chapter 2 Study Guide *continued*

_____ **14.** One of the key habits of mind of scientists is _____, which
allows scientists to expand the boundaries of what we know.
   a. intellectual honesty   **c.** replication
   b. imagination   **d.** correlation

_____ **15.** A road map is an example of a
   a. graphical model.   **c.** conceptual model.
   b. mathematical model.   **d.** physical model.

_____ **16.** Statistics are not used by scientists to
   a. compare data.   **c.** gather data.
   b. analyze data.   **d.** all of the above

_____ **17.** In a scientific investigation, the size of the sample population should
be large enough to
   a. reflect the probability of an unwanted outcome.
   b. give an accurate estimate of the whole population.
   c. closely resemble the system they represent.
   d. all of the above

_____ **18.** If you consider what will add to our understanding of the natural
world in making an environmental decision, you are examining
a(n) _____ value.
   a. ethical/moral   **c.** environmental
   b. aesthetic   **d.** scientific

_____ **19.** What is the first step in an environmental decision-making model?
   a. Explore the consequences of each option.
   b. Consider which values apply to the issue.
   c. Make a decision.
   d. Gather information.

_____ **20.** When you examine a scientific value in making an environmental
decision, you
   a. consider what is right or wrong.
   b. consider what will maintain human health.
   c. use your understanding of the natural world.
   d. think about what will promote learning.

_____ **21.** Which of the following is a possible short-term consequence of
creating a nature preserve?
   a. decrease in habitat destruction
   b. an increase in property values near the preserve
   c. a restriction of recreational activities on private land within
the preserve by state officials
   d. all of the above

Chapter 3: The Dynamic Earth

Study Guide

MATCHING

In the space provided, write the letter of the term or phrase that best matches the description.

_____ **1.** boundary between warm and cold water in an ocean or a lake

_____ **2.** the pieces that compose the lithosphere

_____ **3.** a mountain built from magma

_____ **4.** transfer of energy through space

_____ **5.** water movements in the ocean that are driven by the wind

_____ **6.** layer of Earth between the crust and the core

_____ **7.** a molecule made up of three oxygen atoms

_____ **8.** smaller streams or rivers that flow into larger ones

_____ **9.** the total quantity of dissolved salts in the ocean

_____ **10.** break in Earth's crust

a. mantle

b. ozone

c. fault

d. salinity

e. tributaries

f. tectonic plates

g. thermocline

h. volcano

i. surface currents

j. radiation

MULTIPLE CHOICE

In the space provided, write the letter of the term or phrase that best completes each statement or best answers each question.

_____ **11.** The part of Earth that contains the air we breathe is called the
    a. hydrosphere.
    b. atmosphere.
    c. geosphere.
    d. envirosphere.

_____ **12.** The thin outermost layer of the solid Earth is called the
    a. asthenosphere.
    b. mantle.
    c. outer core.
    d. crust.

_____ **13.** An earthquake of magnitude 5.0 releases how much more energy than an earthquake of magnitude 4.0?
    a. twice the energy
    b. three times the energy
    c. one hundred times the energy
    d. none of the above

Chapter 3 Study Guide *continued*

_____ **14.** Volcanoes occur at tectonic plate boundaries that are
    a. colliding.
    b. slipping past one another.
    c. separating from one another.
    d. both (a) and (c)

_____ **15.** The removal and transport of surface material by wind and water is called
    a. seismicity.
    b. erosion.
    c. tectonics.
    d. vulcanism.

_____ **16.** The stratosphere is the atmospheric layer above the
    a. troposphere.
    b. ionosphere.
    c. mesosphere.
    d. thermosphere.

_____ **17.** Which of the following gases is an important greenhouse gas?
    a. hydrogen
    b. nitrogen
    c. carbon dioxide
    d. oxygen

_____ **18.** The most abundant gas in Earth's atmosphere is
    a. oxygen.
    b. carbon dioxide.
    c. nitrogen.
    d. hydrogen.

_____ **19.** The transfer of heat by air currents (or currents in a liquid) is called
    a. radiation.
    b. conduction.
    c. convection.
    d. condensation.

_____ **20.** The warmest temperature zone of the ocean is the
    a. thermocline.
    b. deep zone.
    c. open ocean.
    d. surface zone.

_____ **21.** Stream-like movements of cold, dense water near the ocean floor are called
    a. surface currents.
    b. deep currents.
    c. bottom currents.
    d. mixing currents.

_____ **22.** One of the most important roles of the ocean is to
    a. add oxygen to the atmosphere.
    b. trap heat near Earth.
    c. regulate temperatures in Earth's atmosphere.
    d. absorb ultraviolet radiation.

_____ **23.** The narrow layer of Earth where life-supporting conditions exist is called the
    a. crust.
    b. surface zone.
    c. troposphere.
    d. biosphere.

_____ **24.** With respect to matter, Earth is mostly
    a. an open system.
    b. a closed system.
    c. an ecosystem.
    d. a biosphere.

_____ **25.** The most important dissolved elements in ocean water are
    a. calcium and magnesium.
    b. calcium and potassium.
    c. calcium and sodium.
    d. sodium and chlorine.

Chapter 4: The Organization of Life

Study Guide

MATCHING

In the space provided, write the letter of the term or phrase that best matches the description.

_____ 1. an individual living thing

_____ 2. a group of various species that live in the same place and interact with each other

_____ 3. living or once living part of an ecosystem

_____ 4. unequal survival and reproduction that results from the presence or absence of particular traits

_____ 5. all the organisms living in an area and their physical environment

_____ 6. change in the genetic characteristics of a population from one generation to the next

_____ 7. all the members of the same species that live in the same place at the same time

_____ 8. nonliving part of an ecosystem

_____ 9. ability of one or more organisms to tolerate a particular chemical designed to kill it

_____ 10. group of organisms that are closely related and that can mate to produce fertile offspring

a. ecosystem

b. population

c. natural selection

d. organism

e. resistance

f. abiotic factor

g. evolution

h. species

i. community

j. biotic factor

MULTIPLE CHOICE

In the space provided, write the letter of the term or phrase that best completes each statement or best answers each question.

_____ 11. What kind of habitat does a salamander need to survive?
   a. damp forest floor
   b. sunny top of a tree
   c. dry forest floor
   d. sunny desert rock

Chapter 4 Study Guide *continued*

_____ **12.** Which of the following king-doms include organisms that can make their own food?
  a. protists and plants
  b. plants and animals
  c. fungi and plants
  d. fungi and protists

_____ **13.** The Chihuahua is a dog that exists because of
  a. natural selection.
  b. artificial selection.
  c. resistance.
  d. abiotic factors.

_____ **14.** Humans have promoted the evolution of insects that are resistant to insecticides by
  a. trying to control pests with chemicals.
  b. using insecticides that are outdated.
  c. using the wrong insecti-cide.
  d. breeding more useful insects.

_____ **15.** Which of the following is *not* true of an adaptation?
  a. It is an advantage to an organism in certain envi-ronments.
  b. It increases an organism's chance of reproducing.
  c. It increases an organism's chance of survival.
  d. It decreases an organ-ism's chance of evolving.

_____ **16.** Which of the following is *not* one of the kingdoms of living things?
  a. Fungi
  b. Bacteria
  c. Animalia
  d. Protista

_____ **17.** One way that bacteria and fungi are important to the environment is that they
  a. produce oxygen.
  b. use the sun's energy to make their own food.
  c. are a major food source in many ecosystems.
  d. break down dead organ-isms.

_____ **18.** Phytoplankton are impor-tant protists because they are the initial source of
  a. food in most land ecosys-tems.
  b. food in most ocean and freshwater ecosystems.
  c. oxygen in the atmo-sphere.
  d. both (a) and (b)

_____ **19.** Many angiosperms depend on
  a. other animals in the oceans.
  b. gymnosperms for repro-ducing.
  c. plants for food.
  d. animals to carry pollen and disperse seeds.

_____ **20.** Which of the following characteristics is shared by bacteria, fungi, and plants?
  a. They usually have cell walls.
  b. They have cell nuclei.
  c. They are single celled.
  d. They have the ability to make their own food.

Chapter 5: How Ecosystems Work
Study Guide

MATCHING

In the space provided, write the letter of the term or phrase that best matches the description.

_____ 1. two types of consumers

_____ 2. a diagram showing the many feeding relationships that are in an ecosystem

_____ 3. the process in which energy from the sun is used by plants to make sugar molecules

_____ 4. illustrates the loss of energy from one trophic level to the next

_____ 5. organisms that get their energy by eating other organisms

_____ 6. stored carbon from the remains of plants and animals that died millions of years ago

_____ 7. organisms that make their own food

_____ 8. change that occurs on an abandoned farm

_____ 9. a part of the carbon cycle

_____ 10. results from excessive use of fertilizers

_____ 11. organisms that transform atmosphereic nitrogen into usable nitrogen compounds

_____ 12. part of the nitrogen cycle

_____ 13. transfer of energy from one organism to another

a. photosynthesis

b. rabbit and coyote

c. fossil fuels

d. producers

e. food web

f. consumers

g. atmospheric CO_2

h. energy pyramid

i. algal bloom

j. atmospheric N_2

k. food chain

l. old-field succession

m. nitrogen-fixing bacteria

MULTIPLE CHOICE

In the space provided, write the letter of the term or phrase that best completes each statement or best answers each question.

_____ 14. What are the first organisms to colonize any newly available area called?
  a. climax species
  b. ferns
  c. pioneer species
  d. mosses

_____ 15. Which of the following is a producer that breaks down rock?
  a. pioneer producer
  b. fungal species
  c. algae
  d. lichen

_____ 16. Humans are affecting the balance of the carbon cycle by
  a. burning fossil fuels.
  b. using carbonates at an alarming rate.
  c. using fertilizers.
  d. replanting the rain forests.

_____ 17. What is a pattern of change that occurs on a surface where an ecosystem has previously existed?
  a. primary succession
  b. secondary succession
  c. tertiary succession
  d. climax community

_____ 18. What do deep-ocean bacteria use to make their food?
  a. the sun
  b. hydrogen sulfide
  c. carbon dioxide
  d. sugar molecules

_____ 19. Which of the following is an herbivore?
  a. cow
  b. lion
  c. bear
  d. grass

_____ 20. Which of the following is a producer?
  a. oak tree
  b. raccoon
  c. cockroach
  d. human

_____ 21. Which of the following is a process in the cell whereby glucose and oxygen produce carbon dioxide, water, and energy?
  a. photosynthesis
  b. cellular respiration
  c. synthesis
  d. decomposition

_____ 22. Which of the following organisms would be found at the top of an energy pyramid?
  a. alga
  b. krill
  c. leopard seal
  d. killer whale

_____ 23. Humans usually get the phosphorus that their bodies need from
  a. eating plants and animals that contain phosphorus.
  b. mining.
  c. food additives.
  d. drinking water.

Chapter 6: Biomes
Study Guide

MATCHING

Match each example in the left column with the appropriate term from the right column.

_____ **1.** regions that have distinctive climates and organisms

_____ **2.** the broad band of coniferous forest located just below the Arctic Circle

_____ **3.** plant with thick, fleshy stems

_____ **4.** sleeping through the dry season

_____ **5.** characterized by dry conditions, short summers, and thin soil

_____ **6.** tropical and subtropical grasslands, wet summers, dry winters

_____ **7.** includes trees and shrubs adapted to shade

_____ **8.** the distance north or south of the equator, measured in degrees

_____ **9.** lies beneath the topsoil of the tundra

_____ **10.** height of an object above sea level

a. latitude

b. understory

c. savanna

d. estivation

e. succulent

f. altitude

g. biomes

h. tundra

i. permafrost

j. taiga

MULTIPLE CHOICE

In the space provided, write the letter of the word or statement that best answers the question or completes the sentence.

_____ **11.** Thin soil, high humidity, and high rainfall represent a
    a. tropical rain forest.
    b. temperate rain forest.
    c. desert.
    d. grassland.

_____ **12.** Birds that migrate during winter, coniferous plants, and cold temperatures represent
    a. the South Pole.
    b. taiga.
    c. a temperate rain forest.
    d. a chaparral.

_____ **13.** The top layer in a tropical rain forest is the
      a. canopy.
      b. understory.
      c. emergent layer.
      d. tree line.

_____ **14.** Extreme temperatures, abundant precipitation, rich, deep soils,
      and a growing season of four to six months represent a
      a. tropical rain forest.
      b. taiga.
      c. temperate deciduous forest.
      d. savanna.

_____ **15.** The biome with the highest species diversity is the
      a. taiga.
      b. tundra.
      c. tropical rain forest.
      d. savanna.

_____ **16.** Hot summers and cold winters, low to moderate rainfall,
      few trees, and rich, fertile soil represent a
      a. tundra.
      b. temperate grassland.
      c. temperate deciduous forest.
      d. desert.

_____ **17.** As you move from the equator toward the North Pole,
      you would be likely to see
      a. rain forests, then deserts, then taiga.
      b. tundra, then deserts, then grasslands.
      c. grasslands, then tundra, then rain forests.
      d. temperate deciduous forests, then taiga, then rain forests.

_____ **18.** Factors that influence where plants grow include
      a. longitude.
      b. climate.
      c. biome maps.
      d. both (a) and (b)

Chapter 7: Aquatic Ecosystems
Study Guide

MATCHING

In the space provided, write the letter of the term or phrase that best matches the description.

_____ 1. wetland dominated by nonwoody plants

_____ 2. precipitation that can carry pollutants into aquatic ecosystems

_____ 3. amount of dissolved salts in water

_____ 4. wetland dominated by woody plants

_____ 5. area where fresh water mixes with salt water

_____ 6. limestone ridges built by tiny animals

_____ 7. located near the bottom of a pond or lake

_____ 8. organisms that break down dead organisms

_____ 9. increase in nutrients in an aquatic ecosystem

_____ 10. aquatic zone found near the shore

_____ 11. threat against a river ecosystem

_____ 12. threat against marine organisms

a. swamp
b. benthic zone
c. dams
d. decomposers
e. littoral zone
f. eutrophication
g. overfishing
h. salinity
i. runoff
j. marsh
k. coral reefs
l. estuary

MULTIPLE CHOICE

In the space provided, write the letter of the term or phrase that best completes each statement or best answers each question.

_____ 13. Estuaries are productive ecosystems because they constantly receive nutrients from
   a. rivers and oceans.
   b. coral reefs.
   c. lakes and ponds.
   d. photosynthesis.

_____ 14. Which of the following is a factor that influences where an organism lives in an aquatic ecosystem?
   a. sunlight
   b. nutrient availability
   c. temperature
   d. all of the above

_____ **15.** In which of the following aquatic ecosystems are both littoral
and benthic zones most likely found?
    a. open ocean
    b. coral reef
    c. lake
    d. none of the above

_____ **16.** What is the source of most ocean pollution?
    a. activities on land
    b. climate changes
    c. aquatic animals
    d. none of the above

_____ **17.** Estuaries
    a. are always saltwater ecosystems.
    b. are always freshwater ecosystems.
    c. are ecosystems where both fresh water and salt water are present.
    d. prevent the development of salt marshes.

_____ **18.** All of the following are examples of saltwater ecosystems except
    a. mangrove swamps.
    b. coral reefs.
    c. salt marshes.
    d. the Florida Everglades.

_____ **19.** One way in which wetlands control flooding is by
    a. filtering out water pollutants.
    b. absorbing water from rivers.
    c. providing habitats for migratory wildlife.
    d. reducing the amount of carbon dioxide released into the air.

_____ **20.** Which of the following is not a threat to coral reefs?
    a. silt runoff
    b. excessive nutrients
    c. growth of algae
    d. zooplankton

Chapter 8: Understanding Populations
Study Guide

MATCHING

In the space provided, write the letter of the term or phrase that best matches the description.

_____ **1.** interaction between two species in which both are harmed

_____ **2.** the functional role of a species within an ecosystem

_____ **3.** one of the three main properties of a population

_____ **4.** development of adaptations as a result of symbiotic relationships

_____ **5.** maximum population that an ecosystem can support indefinitely

_____ **6.** close interaction between two species in which one organism benefits while the other organism is harmed

_____ **7.** the ratio of births to deaths in a population

_____ **8.** maximum number of offspring that each member of a population can produce

_____ **9.** a reduction in population size caused by a natural disaster

_____ **10.** the location where an organism lives

a. density

b. growth rate

c. reproductive potential

d. carrying capacity

e. density independent regulation

f. niche

g. habitat

h. competition

i. parasitism

j. coevolution

MULTIPLE CHOICE

In the space provided, write the letter of the term or phrase that best completes each statement or best answers each question.

_____ **11.** A territory is
   a. a place where one animal lives.
   b. a place where people eat.
   c. an area defended by one or more individuals.
   d. a place for sleeping.

_____ **12.** Which of the following is an example of a parasite?
   a. worm in your intestine   **c.** bee stinger in your arm
   b. a lion hunting zebras   **d.** honeybee on a flower

_____ 13. Bacteria in your intestines are an example of mutualism if they
   a. make you sick.
   b. have no effect on you.
   c. are destroyed by digestive juices.
   d. help you break down food.

_____ 14. Predators_____kill their prey.
   a. always   **c.** never
   b. usually   **d.** try not to

_____ 15. What property of a population may be described as even, clumped, or random?
   a. dispersion   **c.** size
   b. density   **d.** growth rate

_____ 16. What can occur if a population has plenty of food and space, and has no competition or predators?
   a. reduction of carrying capacity   **c.** zero population growth
   b. exponential growth   **d.** coevolution

_____ 17. A grizzly bear can be all of the following *except* a
   a. parasite.   **c.** mutualist.
   b. competitor.   **d.** predator.

_____ 18. The "co-" in coevolution means
   a. apart.   **c.** two.
   b. together.   **d.** predator-prey.

_____ 19. Which of the following has the greatest effect on reproductive potential?
   a. producing more offspring at a time
   b. reproducing more often
   c. having a longer life span
   d. reproducing earlier in life

_____ 20. Members of a species may compete with one another for
   a. running faster.   **c.** giving birth.
   b. social dominance. **d.** mutualism.

_____ 21. A robin that does not affect the tree in which it nests is an example of
   a. parasitism.   **c.** mutualism.
   b. commensalism.   **d.** predation.

_____ 22. Two species can be indirect competitors for food if they
   a. use the same food source at different times.
   b. have different food sources.
   c. fight over food.
   d. eat together peacefully.

Name _____ Class _____ Date _____

Chapter 9: The Human Population
Study Guide

MATCHING

In the space provided, write the letter of the term or phrase that best matches the description.

_____ **1.** highest birth rates

_____ **2.** the distribution of ages in a specific population at a certain time

_____ **3.** percentage of members of a group that are likely to survive to a given age

_____ **4.** movement of individuals out of a population

_____ **5.** the study of populations

_____ **6.** movement of people into cities from rural areas

_____ **7.** the basic facilities and services that support a community

_____ **8.** land that can be used to grow crops

_____ **9.** a model that describes how changes in a population may occur

_____ **10.** average number of children a woman gives birth to in her lifetime

a. demography

b. age structure

c. emigration

d. infrastructure

e. arable land

f. least-developed countries

g. survivorship

h. demographic transition

i. urbanization

j. total fertility rate

MULTIPLE CHOICE

In the space provided, write the letter of the word or statement that best answers the question or completes the sentence.

_____ **11.** The human population doubled from 2 billion to 4 billion people in
  a. about 130 years.
  b. about 44 years.
  c. about 95 years.
  d. about 175 years.

_____ **12.** Some under-developed countries have tried to control population growth by
  a. increasing fertility rate.
  b. decreasing fertility rate.
  c. increasing emigration.
  d. decreasing emigration.

_____ **13.** Suburban sprawl, over-crowded schools, polluted rivers, and inadequate housing are symptoms of
  a. stable population size.
  b. overwhelming population growth.
  c. declining population size.
  d. slow population growth.

_____ **14.** Access to adequate food, clean water, and safe sewage disposal have resulted in a decline in
   a. life expectancy.
   b. the birth rate.
   c. the death rate.
   d. infant health.

_____ **15.** According to the theory of demographic transition, populations in Stage 1 tend to
   a. increase.
   b. decrease.
   c. remain the same.
   d. be large.

_____ **16.** Suburban sprawl results in
   a. traffic jams.
   b. inadequate infrastructure.
   c. reduction of land for farms, ranches, and wildlife habitat.
   d. all of the above

_____ **17.** A population's age structure is represented by a
   a. population pyramid.
   b. survivorship curve.
   c. total fertility rate.
   d. migration rate.

_____ **18.** What is the main source of energy in the poorest countries?
   a. coal
   b. solar collectors
   c. wood
   d. nuclear reactors

_____ **19.** The graph of human population growth since 1200 BCE looks like
   a. a J-curve.
   b. an S-curve.
   c. a horizontal line.
   d. a straight 45° line.

_____ **20.** Infant mortality rates are least effected by
   a. average income.
   b. parents' access to education.
   c. clean water.
   d. adequate food.

_____ **21.** Life expectancy in sub-Saharan Africa has declined due to the epidemic of
   a. tuberculosis.
   b. AIDS.
   c. influenza.
   d. bubonic plague.

_____ **22.** A population will shrink if deaths + emigrants exceeds
   a. deaths + births.
   b. immigration – emigration.
   c. births + immigrants.
   d. the carrying capacity of a nation.

_____ **23.** Which of the following is *not* part of a community's infrastructure?
   a. public water supply
   b. power plants
   c. sewer lines
   d. arable land

_____ **24.** The movement of individuals between areas is called
   a. migration.
   b. life expectancy.
   c. survivorship.
   d. urbanization.

Chapter 10: Biodiversity

Study Guide

MATCHING

In the space provided, write the letter of the term or phrase that best matches the description.

_____ 1. a species that is not native to a particular region

_____ 2. any species that is likely to become endangered if it is not protected

_____ 3. species that are very important to the functioning of an ecosystem

_____ 4. any species whose numbers have fallen so low that it is likely to become extinct in the near future

_____ 5. a species when the very last individual dies

_____ 6. most unknown species belong to this group

_____ 7. growing crops among native plants instead of on cleared land

_____ 8. humans and familiar animals belong to this group

_____ 9. designed to protect groups of species by managing lands in a protected area

_____ 10. critical ecosystems with high species diversity

_____ 11. many antibiotics are derived from chemicals that come from this group

a. keystone species

b. exotic species

c. extinct species

d. endangered species

e. threatened species

f. sustainable land use

g. vertebrates

h. habitat conservation plan

i. insects

j. fungi

k. biodiversity hotspot

Chapter 10 Study Guide *continued*

MULTIPLE CHOICE

In the space provided, write the letter of the term or phrase that best completes each statement or best answers each question.

_____ **12.** Members of a population may be prone to inherited genetic diseases if
  a. the level of genetic diversity of the population is high.
  b. inbreeding takes place frequently within the population.
  c. a variety of habitats are available to the population.
  d. interaction between populations takes place in an ecosystem.

_____ **13.** The human diet has been enriched with native food products such as sweet potatoes, beans, tomatoes, and corn that come from
  a. Pacific islands.
  b. Southwest Asia.
  c. Madagascar and Africa.
  d. Central and South America.

_____ **14.** What level of biodiversity is most commonly equated with the overall concept of biodiversity?
  a. genetic diversity
  b. species diversity
  c. ecosystem diversity
  d. all of the above

_____ **15.** What groups of organisms are most in danger of extinction?
  a. those with small populations
  b. those that migrate or need special habitats
  c. those with large populations that breed quickly
  d. both (a) and (b)

_____ **16.** Which of the following is not one of the ways in which coral reefs are threatened by human activities?
  a. development along waterways
  b. creation of artificial reefs
  c. overharvesting of fish
  d. pollution

_____ **17.** How does preserving biodiversity come into conflict with human interests?
  a. Additional land is used for agriculture or housing in response to population growth.
  b. Species may represent food or a source of income.
  c. both (a) and (b)
  d. none of the above

_____ **18.** Which of the following is not a provision of the Endangered Species Act?
  a. No products from endangered or threatened species may be sold.
  b. Protected plants may be uprooted.
  c. Government projects may not further endanger endangered species.
  d. A species recovery plan must be created.

Chapter 11: Water
Study Guide

MATCHING

In the space provided, write the letter of the term or phrase that best matches the description.

_____ **1.** Mississippi River

_____ **2.** area above an aquifer

_____ **3.** bottled water

_____ **4.** bacteria

_____ **5.** multiple sources

_____ **6.** fertilizer runoff

_____ **7.** law designed to improve water quality

_____ **8.** surface water that percolates through soil

a. pathogen

b. recharge zone

c. nonpoint-source pollution

d. potable

e. watershed

f. artificial eutrophication

g. 1972 Clean Water Act

h. groundwater

MULTIPLE CHOICE

In the space provided, write the letter of the term or phrase that best completes each statement or best answers each question.

_____ **9.** Ninety-seven percent of the world's water resources are found in
    a. fresh water.
    b. salt water.
    c. icecaps and glaciers.
    d. groundwater.

_____ **10.** Earth's surface water is found in
    a. lakes.
    b. rivers.
    c. streams.
    d. all of the above

_____ **11.** Most of the oil that pollutes the ocean comes from
    a. operating boats and personal watercraft.
    b. spills from oil tankers.
    c. runoff from cities and towns.
    d. leaking underground storage facilities.

_____ **12.** The three major global uses of fresh water are
    a. manufacturing goods, wastewater disposal, and irrigation.
    b. drinking, bathing, and growing crops.
    c. drinking, manufacturing goods, and generating power.
    d. residential, agricultural, and industrial uses.

_____13. What is the purpose of adding alum to water during the water treatment process?
  a. to filter and remove large organisms and trash
  b. to form flocs that bacteria and other impurities will cling to
  c. to prevent bacterial growth
  d. to remove unwanted gases

_____14. How is fresh water used in industry?
  a. in manufacturing processes
  b. in the disposal of waste products
  c. to generate power
  d. all of the above

_____15. Many areas of the world that do not have adequate fresh water have become habitable because
  a. rainfall patterns have changed.
  b. water management projects have diverted water to the areas.
  c. icebergs have been towed in to provide fresh water.
  d. people have practiced water conservation.

_____16. A hole that is dug into the ground to obtain fresh water is called
  a. the recharge zone.
  b. a well.
  c. an aquifer.
  d. a watershed.

_____17. Which of the following is one way that a person can conserve water?
  a. Take a bath instead of a shower.
  b. Wash laundry in small, partial loads.
  c. Use a low-flow shower head and take short showers.
  d. Water the lawn daily and at mid-day.

_____18. Which of the following is a source of point-pollution?
  a. unlined landfill
  b. runoff from city streets
  c. precipitation containing air pollution
  d. runoff from farms

_____19. Animal feces would be classified as which type of water pollutant?
  a. pathogens
  b. organic matter
  c. inorganic chemicals
  d. heavy metals

_____20. Polluted groundwater is difficult to clean up because
  a. groundwater is deep in the ground and dispersed through large areas of rock.
  b. pollutants cling to the materials that make up the aquifer and contaminate the clean water.
  c. the recycling process of groundwater can take hundreds or thousands of years.
  d. all of the above

Chapter 12: Air

Study Guide

MATCHING

In the space provided, write the letter of the term or phrase that best matches the description.

_____ **1.** ground-level ozone

_____ **2.** scrubber

_____ **3.** radon gas

_____ **4.** nitrogen oxides

_____ **5.** decreased pH

_____ **6.** possible long-term effect of air pollution

_____ **7.** necessary to control acid precipitation

_____ **8.** atmospheric condition trapping pollution

_____ **9.** possible short-term effect of air pollution

_____ **10.** possible long-term effect of noise pollution

a. primary pollutant

b. secondary pollutant

c. indoor air pollution

d. pollution control

e. acid precipitation

f. temperature inversion

g. lung cancer

h. deafness

i. international agreement

j. nausea

MULTIPLE CHOICE

In the space provided, write the letter of the term or phrase that best completes each statement or best answers each question.

_____ **11.** Which of the following is an example of a primary pollutant?
a. ground-level ozone
b. soot from smoke
c. radon
d. all of the above

_____ **12.** Which of the following would be a potential cause of sick-building syndrome?
a. acid precipitation
b. smog
c. fungi
d. all of the above

Name _____ Class _____ Date _____

Chapter 12 Study Guide *continued*

_____ 13. Catalytic converters, scrubbers, and electrostatic precipitators are examples of
   a. technologies used to treat sick-building syndrome.
   b. technologies used to counteract the effects of acid precipitation on aquatic ecosystems.
   c. technologies used to capture radon gas.
   d. technologies used to control pollution emissions.

_____ 14. During a temperature inversion,
   a. sulfur oxides and nitrogen oxides combine with water in the atmosphere.
   b. an influx of acidic water causes a rapid change in the pH of water.
   c. levels of ground-level ozone decrease.
   d. pollutants are trapped near Earth's surface.

_____ 15. What is *not* a consequence of acid precipitation?
   a. an increase in the pH of soil and water
   b. the death of aquatic plants and animals
   c. the destruction of calcium carbonate in building materials
   d. a change in the balance of soil chemistry

_____ 16. High blood pressure and stress are both human health effects linked to
   a. smog.
   b. air pollution.
   c. light pollution.
   d. noise pollution.

_____ 17. Oil refineries and gasoline stations are both sources of
   a. particulate matter.
   b. volatile organic compounds.
   c. smog.
   d. all of the above

_____ 18. Uranium-bearing rocks underneath a house can be a source of
   a. ozone.
   b. asbestos.
   c. radon.
   d. formaldehyde.

_____ 19. An increase in the pH of a lake would most likely indicate
   a. the lake suffers from acid shock.
   b. calcium carbonate has been released into the lake.
   c. the area in which the lake is located suffers from acid precipitation.
   d. higher than average sulfur oxide levels in the atmosphere.

_____ 20. Acid precipitation is formed when
   a. sulfur oxides or nitrogen oxides combine with water.
   b. sulfur oxides combine with nitrogen oxides.
   c. ozone combines with automobile exhaust.
   d. nitric or sulfuric acids combine with ozone.

Name _____ Class _____ Date _____

Study Guide

MATCHING

In the space provided, write the letter of the term or phrase that best matches the description.

_____ 1. international agreement to limit CFC production

_____ 2. destroyed by CFCs

_____ 3. caused by wind and influenced by Earth's rotation

_____ 4. increases when fossil fuels are burned

_____ 5. low-angle sunlight

_____ 6. winds push warm water eastward in the Pacific Ocean

_____ 7. heat trapped by atmosphere near Earth's surface

_____ 8. potential result of high UV radiation at Earth's surface

_____ 9. water is cooler than usual in the eastern Pacific Ocean

_____ 10. trade winds, westerlies, and polar easterlies

a. El Niño

b. atmospheric CO_2

c. stratospheric ozone

d. winter

e. Montreal Protocol

f. greenhouse effect

g. DNA damage

h. surface ocean currents

i. prevailing winds

j. La Niña

MULTIPLE CHOICE

In the space provided, write the letter of the term or phrase that best completes each statement or best answers each question.

_____ 11. Climate in a region is
a. the long-term prevailing atmospheric conditions.
b. determined only by seasonal daylight hours.
c. the atmospheric conditions on a given day.
d. never affected by ocean currents.

_____ 12. Rain frequently results whenever
a. cold, moist air rises.
b. warm, moist air rises.
c. warm, dry air sinks.
d. cold, dry air sinks.

_____ **13.** Latitude strongly influences climate because _____ solar energy falls on areas that are closer to the equator than to the poles.
  a. less
  b. the same amount of
  c. more
  d. sometimes less

_____ **14.** An important property of air circulation is
  a. warm air is denser than cold air.
  b. cold air and warm air have the same density.
  c. cold air is denser than warm air.
  d. air has no mass.

_____ **15.** Which of the following gases is *most* responsible for the greenhouse effect?
  a. nitrous oxide
  b. methane
  c. oxygen
  d. water vapor

_____ **16.** Which of the following reduce(s) CO_2 in the atmosphere?
  a. phytoplankton
  b. tropical rain forests
  c. oceans
  d. all of the above

_____ **17.** During the summer, sunlight in the Northern Hemisphere shines
  a. obliquely for long days.
  b. slanting for short days.
  c. more directly for long days.
  d. less directly for short days.

_____ **18.** Ozone in the stratosphere
  a. causes skin cancer.
  b. prevents DNA repair.
  c. absorbs UV light.
  d. destroys CFCs.

_____ **19.** Ozone holes appear in polar regions during springtime when ozone-destroying
  a. chlorine atoms are released from polar stratospheric clouds.
  b. chlorine atoms are captured by polar stratospheric clouds.
  c. CFCs are synthesized on polar stratospheric clouds.
  d. CFCs magnify ultraviolet light.

_____ **20.** Once in the atmosphere, CFCs
  a. quickly become harmless.
  b. destroy ozone for only a short time.
  c. persist but stop destroying ozone.
  d. persist and continue to destroy ozone for decades.

_____ **21.** La Niña is the _____ phase of the El Niño-Southern Oscillation cycle.
  a. warm   **c.** neutral
  b. cold   **d.** mixing

_____ **22.** The average global temperature has _____ during the 20th century.
  a. remained the same
  b. increased every year
  c. risen some years and fallen other years but has increased overall
  d. risen some years and fallen other years but has decreased overall

Chapter 14: Land
Study Guide

MATCHING

In the space provided, write the letter of the term or phrase that best matches the description.

_____ 1. damaged rangeland

_____ 2. protected land

_____ 3. purified water

_____ 4. bridges

_____ 5. low population density

_____ 6. development

_____ 7. clear-cutting

_____ 8. rangeland and urban land

a. infrastructure

b. urbanization

c. deforestation

d. rural

e. wilderness

f. ecosystem services

g. overgrazing

h. human uses of land

MULTIPLE CHOICE

In the space provided, write the letter of the word or statement that best answers the question or completes the sentence.

_____ 9. Land that contains relatively few people and large areas of open space is considered
    a. rural.
    b. urban.
    c. suburban.
    d. rangelands.

_____ 10. All of the following is allowed in wilderness *except*
    a. research.
    b. camping.
    c. development.
    d. fishing.

_____ 11. The timber industry classifies forestlands into three categories called
    a. oftwoods, hardwoods, and mixed woods.
    b. pine, redwood, and mixed.
    c. evergreen, deciduous, and mixed.
    d. virgin forest, native forest, and tree farms.

_____ **12.** A heat island can
   a. affect weather patterns over a city.
   b. reduce the average temperatures in a city.
   c. absorb less heat than vegetation.
   d. have a lower temperature than the surrounding countryside.

_____ **13.** Tree harvesting methods include
   a. selective cutting.
   b. reforestation.
   c. clear-cutting.
   d. both (a) and (c)

_____ **14.** A fire station is an example of
   a. infrastructure.
   b. suburbanization.
   c. land-use planning.
   d. renovation.

_____ **15.** Which of the following is *not* a method of preventing overgrazing?
   a. limiting herd size
   b. rotating the breed of cattle
   c. removing herds to allow vegetation to recover
   d. replanting native vegetation

_____ **16.** Which of the following is *not* an environmental benefit of open spaces?
   a. moderation of temperatures
   b. absorption of rainwater runoff
   c. provision of aesthetic value
   d. source of lumber for homes

_____ **17.** Which of the following is a benefit of preserving farmland?
   a. prime locations for home sites
   b. soil erosion protection
   c. productive land for growing crops
   d. a greenbelt for crowded urban areas

_____ **18.** Which of the following uses the largest amount of land in
   the United States?
   a. forestland
   b. rangeland and pasture
   c. cropland
   d. parks and preserves

Chapter 15: Food and Agriculture

Study Guide

MATCHING

In the space provided, write the letter of the term or phrase that best matches the description.

_____ **1.** crop is harvested without turning over the soil

_____ **2.** causes resistance to pesticides

_____ **3.** almost entirely a result of poverty

_____ **4.** desirable traits transferred

_____ **5.** used to transfer desirable traits

_____ **6.** soil that can support the growth of healthy plants

_____ **7.** characterized by new crop varieties, increased yields

_____ **8.** the goal is to minimize economic damage from pests

_____ **9.** results in depleted fish populations

_____ **10.** salinization

a. green revolution

b. overuse of land

c. fertile soil

d. high pesticide use

e. integrated pest management

f. no-till farming

g. accumulation of salts in soil

h. genetic engineering

i. overharvesting

j. malnutrition

MULTIPLE CHOICE

In the space provided, write the letter of the term or phrase that best completes each statement or best answers each question.

_____ **11.** A given plot of land can produce more food when used to grow plants than when used to raise animals because
   a. 1 Cal animal protein requires 10 Cal from plants.
   b. one-tenth of a plant's mass can be used as food.
   c. plants provide more nutrients per gram.
   d. both (a) and (b)

_____ **12.** The green revolution depended on
   a. new biodegradable pesticides.
   b. high-yielding grain varieties.
   c. clearing forest for crop land.
   d. organic fertilizers.

_____ **13.** Most of the living organisms in fertile soil are found in
    a. the surface litter and topsoil.
    b. the leaching zone.
    c. the subsoil.
    d. the bedrock.

_____ **14.** Erosion is a danger whenever the soil is
    a. bare and exposed to wind and rain.
    b. plowed along the contour of the land.
    c. covered with grass.
    d. covered by forest.

_____ **15.** The development of pesticide resistance is an example of
    a. malnutrition.
    b. persistence.
    c. pest control.
    d. evolution.

_____ **16.** All of the following describe typical types of malnutrition *except*
    a. amino acid deficiency.
    b. insufficient variety of foods.
    c. diet of mostly vegetables and grains.
    d. low Calorie consumption.

_____ **17.** Livestock in developing countries provide
    a. manure.
    b. eggs and meat.
    c. leather and wool.
    d. all of the above

_____ **18.** Biological pest control aims to do all the following *except*
    a. maintain tolerable pest levels.
    b. reduce all insects to low levels.
    c. leave non-pest species unharmed.
    d. boost plants' natural defenses.

_____ **19.** Plowing with machines, irrigating with drip systems, and _____ are all modern agricultural methods.
    a. using manure
    b. applying chemical fertilizers
    c. irrigating with ditches
    d. both (a) and (b)

_____ **20.** Earth's available arable land is being reduced by
    a. fast-growing human populations.
    b. soil erosion.
    c. desertification.
    d. all of the above

_____ **21.** All of these contribute to famine *except*
    a. crop failure.
    b. green revolution.
    c. unequal distribution of food.
    d. drought.

_____ **22.** Almost _____ of the seafood consumed in the world is produced through aquaculture.
    a. one-half
    b. one-third
    c. one-fourth
    d. three-fourths

Chapter 16: Mining and Mineral Resources

Study Guide

MATCHING

Write the letter of the term or phrase on the right that best matches the description on the left in the space provided.

_____ 1. process of returning land to its original or better condition after mining

_____ 2. the wall of a coal seam

_____ 3. minerals that contain valuable substances

_____ 4. two or more metals that are combined

_____ 5. open pit used to mine materials near the surface

_____ 6. process by which crushed ore is melted at high temperatures to separate impurities from molten metal

_____ 7. mining method used when ore deposits are located close to Earth's surface

_____ 8. sand, gravel, and crushed rock

_____ 9. minerals concentrated by wind and water movement into surface deposits

_____ 10. the sinking of regions of the ground with little or no horizontal movement

a. alloy

b. surface mining

c. long wall

d. subsidence

e. ore minerals

f. aggregates

g. reclamation

h. quarry

i. smelting

j. placer deposits

MULTIPLE CHOICE

In the space provided, write the letter of the term or phrase that best completes each statement or best answers each question.

_____ 11. The first step in surface coal mining is
   a. to remove and set aside the soil that covers the area to be mined.
   b. to use heavy equipment to take core samples.
   c. to test to see if quarrying would be more effective.
   d. to make cuts in the coal for easier removal.

_____ 12. A serious hazard of coal mining is
   a. a high-pressure water blast.
   b. an aggregation.
   c. excess overburden.
   d. an underground mine fire.

_____ **13.** Dredging streambeds may be an effective technique for mining
    a. silica.
    b. coal.
    c. gold.
    d. sulfur.

_____ **14.** Before mining a site, a mining company must do all of the following *except*
    a. obtain permits from state agencies.
    b. comply with federal regulations.
    c. obtain bonding.
    d. cut into a section of the longwall.

_____ **15.** What is the arrangement of atoms in a mineral?
    a. porous, woven patterns
    b. regular, repeating geometric patterns
    c. irregular patterns
    d. clumped groups of like elements

_____ **16.** Nonmetallic minerals prized mainly for their beauty, rarity, or durability are called
    a. aggregates.
    b. overburden.
    c. native elements.
    d. gemstones.

_____ **17.** Which of the following is *not* affected when soil is removed from a surface mine?
    a. plant life
    b. soil nutrients
    c. animal habitat
    d. deep coal seams

_____ **18.** Mining companies can identify areas of valuable mineral resources by
    a. mineral exploration.
    b. smelting.
    c. mineral excavation.
    d. dredging.

_____ **19.** Solar evaporation is practical in order to obtain salt from sea water in climates where rainfall is exceeded by
    a. evaporation.
    b. snowfall.
    c. high-speed winds.
    d. humidity.

_____ **20.** Which of the following is *not* a way that ore minerals may form?
    a. cooling of magma
    b. circulation of hydrothermal solutions through rocks
    c. flooding of empty streambeds and rivers
    d. evaporation of water that contains salts

_____ **21.** Which of the following is one reason why undersea mining has been largely unsuccessful to date?
    a. Deposits at great water depths are difficult to work.
    b. Ocean water is too salty.
    c. There is too much aggregate on the ocean floor.
    d. Magma exists under the ocean floor.

Chapter 17: Nonrenewable Energy
Study Guide

MATCHING

In the space provided, write the letter of the term or phrase that best matches the description.

_____ 1. fossil fuels

_____ 2. region with the most coal deposits

_____ 3. electric generator

_____ 4. site of world's worst nuclear reactor accident

_____ 5. nuclear energy

_____ 6. used in a nuclear reaction

_____ 7. made from petroleum

_____ 8. region with the most oil deposits

_____ 9. used in nuclear fusion

_____ 10. region with the most natural gas deposits

a. Middle East

b. fission and fusion

c. oil, natural gas, and coal

d. magnetic fields and rotating turbines

e. gasoline and plastics

f. Asia

g. uranium

h. Chernobyl

i. Europe

j. deuterium and tritium

MULTIPLE CHOICE

In the space provided, write the letter of the term or phrase that best completes each statement or best answers each question.

_____ 11. Which of the following is *not* a main use of fuel?
a. transportation
b. manufacturing
c. heating and cooling buildings
d. cooking

_____ 12. The energy in fossil fuels is often converted into
a. electricity.
b. magnetic fields.
c. uranium.
d. power plants.

_____ 13. Which country uses the least amount of energy per person?
a. Argentina
b. Japan
c. United States
d. Canada

_____ 14. Much of the oil and natural gas in the United States is located in
a. Alaska, Minnesota, New York, and Texas.
b. Alaska, California, Michigan, and Nevada.
c. Texas, Colorado, New York, and the Gulf of Mexico.
d. Alaska, Texas, California, and the Gulf of Mexico.

Name _____ Class _____ Date _____

_____ **15.** Most of the world's fossil fuel reserves are made up of
    a. oil.   **c.** coal.
    b. natural gas.   **d.** waste rock.

_____ **16.** Crude oil is another name for
    a. fossil fuel.   **c.** petroleum.
    b. natural gas.   **d.** methane.

_____ **17.** Internal combustion engines release
    a. carbon dioxide into the atmosphere.
    b. nuclear waste into the atmosphere.
    c. iodized oil into the atmosphere.
    d. methane into the atmosphere.

_____ **18.** Oil production is still increasing, but it
    a. will start decreasing in the next year.
    b. is increasing much more dramatically than it did in the past.
    c. will start decreasing in the next five years.
    d. is increasing much more slowly than it did in the 1960s.

_____ **19.** A large oil reserve
    a. was discovered in Morocco in the year 2000.
    b. has not been discovered in the past decade.
    c. has only been discovered in Saudi Arabia.
    d. will probably be discovered on the moon.

_____ **20.** Which of the following is *not* a consequence of using nuclear energy?
    a. production of electricity
    b. reduction in the use of fossil fuels
    c. a safer environment for humans
    d. release of less radioactivity into the atmosphere than burning coal

_____ **21.** Nuclear fusion and nuclear fission are different because
    a. fusion releases no energy.
    b. fission is a consequence of fusion.
    c. nuclei unite during fusion and split during fission.
    d. fission does not produce nuclear waste.

_____ **22.** Which of the following is *not* true?
    a. Uranium-bearing rocks are in unlimited supply.
    b. Building and maintaining a safe reactor is very expensive.
    c. It is difficult to find a safe place to store nuclear waste.
    d. The fission process can get out of control.

_____ **23.** The most serious nuclear accident in the United States occurred at
    a. Chernobyl.   **c.** Diablo Canyon.
    b. Yucca Mountain. **d.** Three Mile Island.

Chapter 18: Renewable Energy
Study Guide

MATCHING

In the space provided, write the letter of the term or phrase that best matches the description.

_____ **1.** plant material, manure, and wood

_____ **2.** uses collectors with moving parts to capture the sun's energy

_____ **3.** saves energy

_____ **4.** energy sources that are still in development

_____ **5.** energy produced from moving water

_____ **6.** uses the sun's energy to heat something directly, without moving parts

_____ **7.** energy from heat in Earth's interior

_____ **8.** uses low pressure and warm ocean water to boil colder ocean water

_____ **9.** percentage of energy that does useful work in a system

_____ **10.** uses hydrogen as an energy source

a. passive solar heating

b. ocean thermal energy conversion (OTEC)

c. alternative energy

d. biomass fuel

e. fuel cell

f. active solar heating

g. energy efficiency

h. energy conservation

i. hydroelectric energy

j. geothermal energy

MULTIPLE CHOICE

In the space provided, write the letter of the term or phrase that best completes each statement or best answers each question.

_____ **11.** Wind, moving water, sunlight, and heat from Earth's interior are sources of
    a. alternative energy.
    b. geothermal energy.
    c. renewable energy.
    d. ocean thermal energy

_____ **12.** Which of the following uses solar collectors to heat water?
    a. passive solar heating
    b. active solar heating
    c. photovoltaic cells
    d. all of the above

_____ **13.** Which of the following is the fastest-growing source of energy in the world?
    a. passive solar heating
    b. photovoltaic cells
    c. fuel cells
    d. wind power

_____ **14.** Which of the following is a major source of biomass fuel in developing countries?
    a. wood
    b. dung
    c. corn
    d. both (a) and (b)

_____ **15.** A geothermal power plant gets energy by
    a. pumping heated water or steam from rock formations.
    b. circulating fluid underground.
    c. holding water behind a dam.
    d. using methane from decomposition.

_____ **16.** Tidal power, hydrogen fuel cells, and ocean thermal energy conversion are sources of
    a. alternative energy.
    b. geothermal energy.
    c. nonrenewable energy.
    d. hydroelectric energy.

_____ **17.** Which of the following descriptions of hybrid cars is correct?
    a. Hybrid cars do not use gasoline engines.
    b. Hybrid cars have not been made yet.
    c. Hybrid cars are energy-efficient.
    d. Hybrid cars rely on biomass fuel.

_____ **18.** Which of the following statements about hydrogen as a fuel source is correct?
    a. The amount of hydrogen on Earth is too small to meet our fuel needs.
    b. Hydrogen can be burned as a fuel or used to produce electricity chemically.
    c. When hydrogen is burned, it releases pollutants.
    d. Generating hydrogen by burning fossil fuels is inexpensive.

_____ **19.** Sunlight falls on a semiconductor, causing it to release electrons, in a
    a. photovoltaic cell.
    b. fuel cell.
    c. battery.
    d. solar collector.

_____ **20.** People can conserve energy in their daily lives by driving a vehicle
    a. mostly for short distances.
    b. instead of taking a bus or train.
    c. with a large gas tank.
    d. that is fuel-efficient.

Chapter 19: Waste
Study Guide

MATCHING

In the space provided, write the letter of the term or phrase that best matches the description.

_____ 1. any discarded solid material

_____ 2. can be broken down by biological processes

_____ 3. requires producers of hazardous waste to keep records of how wastes are handled

_____ 4. place to dispose of waste by burying it

_____ 5. water that contains dissolved chemicals from wastes that have been buried

a. compost

b. biodegradable

c. landfill

d. solid waste

e. hazardous waste

f. Resource Conservation and Recovery Act (RCRA)

g. incinerator

h. mining waste

i. leachate

j. surface impoundment

_____ 6. rocks and minerals left over from excavation and processing

_____ 7. facility for burning trash

_____ 8. nutrient-rich material made from decomposed plant and animal materials

_____ 9. any toxic, corrosive, or explosive waste

_____ 10. process used for disposing of wastes involving a pond with a sealed bottom

MULTIPLE CHOICE

In the space provided, write the letter of the word or statement that best answers the question or completes the sentence.

_____ 11. Solid waste includes all of the following *except*
  a. agricultural waste.   **c.** plastics.
  b. methane.   **d.** food waste.

_____ 12. The ash produced when solid waste is incinerated is _____ than the original solid waste.
  a. less toxic   **c.** as toxic
  b. more toxic   **d.** more recyclable

Chapter 19 Study Guide *continued*

_____ **13.** If an owner of a business illegally dumps hazardous waste, which law allows the EPA to sue the owner and force the owner to pay for the cleanup?
  a. the Superfund Act
  b. the Incinerator Act
  c. RCRA
  d. the Love Canal Act

_____ **14.** Surface impoundment includes which physical process?
  a. decontamination
  b. evaporation
  c. injection
  d. all of the above

_____ **15.** One disadvantage of biodegradable plastic is that
  a. it has to be blended with plant sugars in order to be useful.
  b. it has to be left in the sun for months before it can begin to degrade.
  c. it is toxic and useful only in industry.
  d. the plastic parts are reduced to smaller pieces but are not completely degraded.

_____ **16.** Which regulation requires producers of hazardous wastes to document how their wastes are handled?
  a. the Superfund Act
  b. the Resource Conservation and Recovery Act
  c. the United States Environmental Protection Agency (EPA)
  d. the Love Canal Act

_____ **17.** Which of the following is the most important function of a landfill?
  a. to provide leachate for other industrial processes
  b. to contain buried waste and prevent it from contaminating the environment.
  c. to be as inexpensive as possible to build
  d. all of the above

_____ **18.** Which of the following would *not* reduce the amount of municipal solid waste going to landfills?
  a. composting yard waste
  b. eliminating recycling programs
  c. reusing products
  d. all of the above

Chapter 20: The Environment and Human Health
Study Guide

MATCHING

In the space provided, write the letter of the term or phrase that best matches the description.

_____ 1. organism that causes disease

_____ 2. study of the harmful effects of substances on organisms

_____ 3. study of the spread of disease

_____ 4. particles in the air that are small enough to breathe into the lungs

_____ 5. amount of a particular chemical to which a person is exposed

_____ 6. transmitter of a disease to people

_____ 7. organism in which a pathogen lives all or part of its life

_____ 8. estimate of the risk posed by an action or substance

_____ 9. previously unknown cause of disease

_____ 10. shows the relative effect of various doses of a drug or chemical on an organism

a. toxicology

b. dose

c. dose-response curve

d. epidemiology

e. risk assessment

f. particulates

g. pathogen

h. host

i. vector

j. emerging virus

MULTIPLE CHOICE

In the space provided, write the letter of the term or phrase that best completes each statement or best answers each question.

_____ 11. Which of the following pollutants is used in agriculture and landscaping and might cause nerve damage, birth defects, and cancer in humans?
   a. particulate matter
   b. lead
   c. pesticides
   d. bacteria

_____ 12. Which of the following pollutants is found in old paint and gasoline and can cause brain damage and learning problems?
   a. particulate matter
   b. lead
   c. coal dust
   d. pesticides

Name _____ Class _____ Date _____

_____ 13. Toxicology is used
to determine
   a. the classification of
a pathogen.
   b. the vectors of a disease.
   c. how harmful a
substance is.
   d. what emerging viruses
cause disease.

_____ 14. After an outbreak of an
illness, scientists use
epidemiology to try to find
   a. the origin of the disease.
   b. how the disease spreads.
   c. how to prevent the
disease from spreading.
   d. All of the above

_____ 15. Radon, a pollutant that
causes cancer, comes from
   a. cigarette smoke.
   b. granite bedrock.
   c. processed foods.
   d. drinking water.

_____ 16. What percentage of com-
mercial chemicals have
been tested for toxicity?
   a. 10 percent
   b. 30 percent
   c. 50 percent
   d. 90 percent

_____ 17. Which of the following
statements is correct?
   a. Landfills solved pollution problems caused by
waste disposal.
   b. Wastewater from
cities no longer carries
toxic chemicals into
waterways.

   c. Laws regulating waste
disposal have put an end
to pollution problems
caused by wastes.
   d. Much of the pollution
in our environment is a
byproduct of inadequate
waste disposal.

_____ 18. The environment is an
important factor in the
spread of cholera and
dysentery because
   a. air can carry the
pathogens.
   b. water provides a habitat
in which the pathogens
breed.
   c. the pathogens reproduce
in soil.
   d. the disease is transmitted
by mosquitoes.

_____ 19. Which of the following
environmental changes is
most likely to lead to the
spread of parasites such as
hookworm?
   a. overuse of pesticides
   b. global warming
   c. overuse of antibiotics
   d. soil erosion

_____ 20. Which of the following is an
emerging virus?
   a. West Nile
   b. measles
   c. diphtheria
   d. schistosomiasis

Chapter 21: Economics, Policy, and the Future
Study Guide

MATCHING

In the space provided, write the letter of the term or phrase that best matches the description.

_____ 1. when environmental and social conditions are linked worldwide

_____ 2. allows individuals to affect environmental policy

_____ 3. increase in the flow of money and products within a market

_____ 4. document that assesses the environmental impact of projects or policies

_____ 5. resulted in Agenda 21—a plan to address a range of environmental issues while allowing economic growth

_____ 6. enforces Endangered Species Act

_____ 7. self-contained economic systems

_____ 8. organized attempt to influence lawmakers' decisions

_____ 9. payment for actions that benefit society

_____ 10. economists view these as market failures

_____ 11. the study of the choices people make as they use and distribute limited resources

_____ 12. leader in the conservation of natural areas

_____ 13. resulted in an agreement to reduce global emissions of greenhouse gases

_____ 14. Paul Ehrlich was its author

_____ 15. something individuals can do to help the environment

_____ 16. Rachel Carson was its author

a. markets
b. Earth Summit of 1992
c. economics
d. *The Population Bomb*
e. *Silent Spring*
f. globalization
g. lobbying
h. recycling
i. voting
j. economic incentive
k. Kyoto Protocol
l. Environmental Impact Statement
m. environmental problems
n. economic growth
o. U.S. Fish and Wildlife Service
p. Theodore Roosevelt

Chapter 21 Study Guide *continued*

MULTIPLE CHOICE

In the space provided, write the letter of the term or phrase that best completes each statement or best answers each question.

_____ **17.** Which tends to be most responsive to citizen input?
  a. local government
  b. state government
  c. federal government
  d. an international agency

_____ **18.** Which is *not* an international environmental agreement?
  a. Agenda 21
  b. Kyoto Protocol
  c. EIS
  d. Law of the Sea

_____ **19.** Which of the following is an example of a private effort to help the environment?
  a. An individual donates money for a park.
  b. A business recycles its waste.
  c. A nonprofit group buys land for preservation.
  d. all of the above

_____ **20.** What factors can limit the usefulness of television news as a source of information on environmental issues?
  a. News reports are brief.
  b. News reports may leave out information.
  c. The information comes from only one source.
  d. all of the above

_____ **21.** It is difficult to achieve global sustainability because
  a. it is an unrealistic goal.
  b. governments do not always agree on how to solve environmental problems.

  c. international agreements are not binding.
  d. globalization is increasing.

_____ **22.** What is the Nature Conservancy?
  a. an organization that collects resources to buy land and establishes nature preserves
  b. an organization that rescues endangered species
  c. an organization that runs breeding programs for endangered species
  d. an agency of the EPA that manages wilderness areas

_____ **23.** Economic systems _____ natural systems.
  a. operate within
  b. are independent of
  c. have no relation to
  d. are equal to

_____ **24.** A policy that rewards a company financially for reducing the amount of waste produced is an example of
  a. the relationship between economics and the environment.
  b. an economic incentive.
  c. economic growth.
  d. globalization.